MW00892671

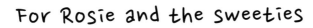

For Rosie and the sweeties

This is a work of fiction. Names, characters, places, and incidents either are the product of the author's imagination or are used fictitiously. Any resemblance to actual persons, living or dead, events, or locales is entirely coincidental.

copyright © 2024 by Matthew Balleza

All rights reserved. No part of this book may be reproduced or used in any manner without written permission of the copyright owner except for the use of quotations in a book review.

First edition February 2024

www.mattballeza.com

CHALKSY

written and illustrated by:
Matthew Balleza

There once was a school where
students took school very seriously.

Every day they arrived
sharp at 7 am.

With their homework done,

And their lunches packed,

And their socks pulled high,

And their backpacks stuffed—

So stuffed, that if they fell
they could not get back up...

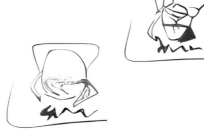

And all day long they kept busy.

There were always bells ringing, pencils scribbling, and little feet staying on straight silver lines—

Going patter, patter, patter, patter...to their next thing.

The Principal, Mr. Crupps, liked it this way.

He liked school neat and orderly and busy.

Some days he would poke his nose out of his office and say:

AHHH...it smells like learning today!

But not everyone liked the learning smells or the busy bells or staying on lines or socks pulled high—

And one day, someone rebelled...

At recess a teacher found a group of students making a commotion.

They were laughing at a picture of Mr. Crupps with clocks for eyes.

The picture was signed, chalksy.

Chalksy

chalksy!?

who's chalksy? the
teacher said.

But no one knew.

Soon there were more
pictures, more every day.

Here and there they appeared
- up high and down low.

The hallway lines disappeared,
replaced by lava flow.

Some were big,

Some were small,

Some were pigs on bathroom stalls.

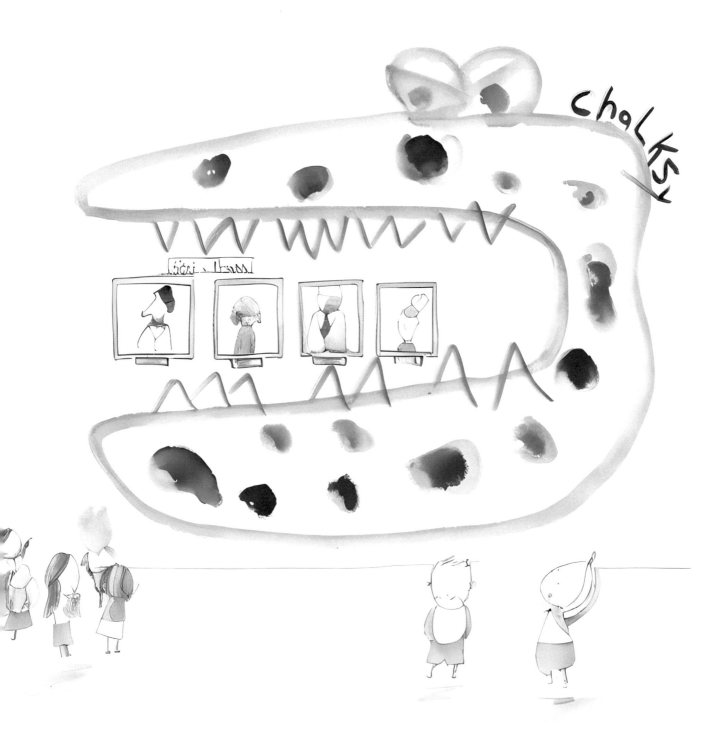

Others had teeth...

And some were hairy,

Some were rather ordinary.

But all of them made
the students stop and
look, bend their heads,
and drop their books.

Some of the students were so inspired they began to make their own.

All the while, Mr. Crupps waited and watched.

After a long time, Mr. Crupps had enough.

He called an assembly.

Waving and yelling and stomping his foot,
he declared,

I've seen enough, I've seen it all, enough
with the drawings all over the walls!

Do you think learning means silliness and doodles and purple-haired poodles?

There's chalk everywhere, the school is a mess. Which one of you is chalksy! You better confess...

As he looked out over the crowd,
suddenly Jenny F. stood up and said,

Then Jenny S. said,

NO...I AM CHALKSY!

Then the winkle brothers said,

NO... WE'RE CHALKSY!

Soon the whole auditorium
was bustling with chalksys.

E-nough!! Mr. Crupps said,
and the room fell hush.

Because whoever thinks
they're chalksy are...

I've been reminded of something so stupendous it musn't be missed.

School's not just schedules and tests and getting good grades.

It means color and pizzazz and learning to play.

And from that day forward things changed.

The bells were a little less busy, and the
hallways lines a little less straight.

And the students took school with a little
more...

Play.

But they never found chalksy to this day...

Made in the USA
Columbia, SC
24 September 2024

42983370R00033